Hello, America!

Empire State Building

by Katherine Rawson

Bullfrog Books

Ideas for Parents and Teachers

Bullfrog Books let children practice reading informational text at the earliest reading levels. Repetition, familiar words, and photo labels support early readers.

Before Reading

- Discuss the cover photo. What does it tell them?

- Look at the picture glossary together. Read and discuss the words.

Read the Book

- "Walk" through the book and look at the photos. Let the child ask questions. Point out the photo labels.

- Read the book to the child, or have him or her read independently.

After Reading

- Prompt the child to think more. Ask: What is the tallest building you have visited? How tall was it? Did you ride an elevator?

Bullfrog Books are published by Jump!
5357 Penn Avenue South
Minneapolis, MN 55419
www.jumplibrary.com

Library of Congress Cataloging-in-Publication Data

Names: Rawson, Katherine, author.
Title: Empire State Building / by Katherine Rawson.
Description: Minneapolis, MN: Jump!, Inc., 2018.
"Bullfrog Books." | Includes index.
Identifiers: LCCN 2017020655 (print)
LCCN 2017021130 (ebook)
ISBN 9781624966576 (e-book)
ISBN 9781620318621 (hard cover: alk. paper)
Subjects: LCSH: Empire State Building (New York, N.Y.)—Juvenile literature. | New York (N.Y.)—Buildings, structures, etc.—Juvenile literature.
Classification: LCC F128.8.E46 (ebook)
LCC F128.8.E46 R39 2017 (print) | DDC 974.7/1—dc23
LC record available at https://lccn.loc.gov/2017020655

Editor: Kirsten Chang
Book Designer: Molly Ballanger
Photo Researcher: Molly Ballanger

Photo Credits: Tetra Images/SuperStock, cover; pisaphotography/Shutterstock, 1, 5, 23tr; GraphicaArtis/Getty, 3; Shawn Kashou/Shutterstock, 4, 23br; SZ Photo/Scherl/Alamy, 6–7; Print Collector/Getty, 8–9; Bettmann/Getty, 10–11; travelview/Shutterstock, 12, 23tl; DavidMelian/iStock, 13; Antonio Gravante/Dreamstime, 14–15; Roman Tiraspolsky/Shutterstock, 16–17; zhu difeng/Shutterstock, 18, 23ml; Atlantide Phototravel/Getty, 19; Giuliano Del Moretto/Shutterstock, 20–21; Monkey Business Images/Shutterstock, 20–21; PixelSquid3d/Shutterstock, 22; Icatnews/Shutterstock, 23bl; 3RUS/Shutterstock, 23mr; Chris Howey/Shutterstock, 24.

Printed in the United States of America at Corporate Graphics in North Mankato, Minnesota.

Table of Contents

Very Tall

Look up.

It is the Empire State Building.

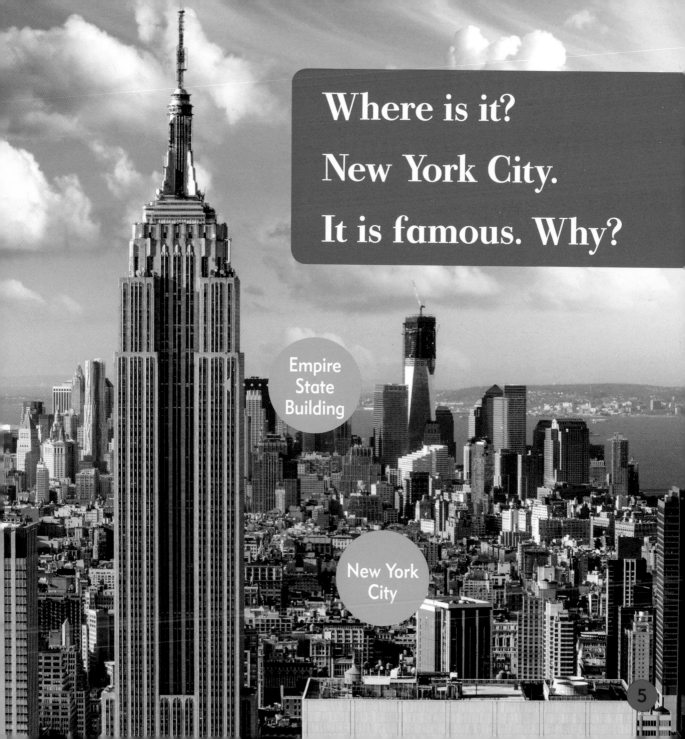

Where is it?
New York City.
It is famous. Why?

Empire State Building

New York City

5

It was 1930.

Times were tough.

But they built this
building anyway.

It was beautiful.

It was strong.

People loved it.

It brought them hope.

It opened in 1931.

It was the tallest building in the world.

It was a symbol of America's strength in hard times.

EMPIRE STATE

11

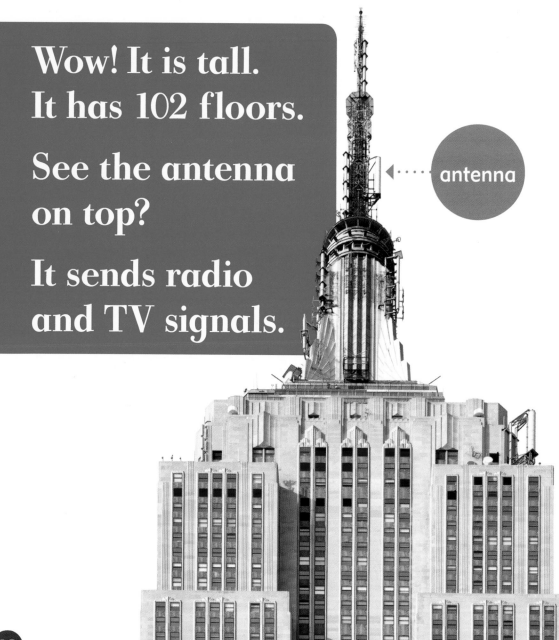

Wow! It is tall.
It has 102 floors.

See the antenna
on top?

It sends radio
and TV signals.

antenna

At night, it lights up.
It can be many colors.

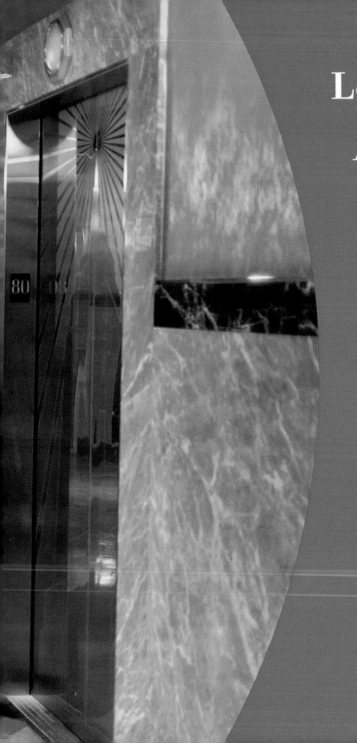

Let's go in.

An elevator
takes us up.

It goes fast.

It takes less
than a minute.

See all the people!

We use binoculars.

The day is clear.

We can see five states.

We take pictures.

We had a fun visit!

How Tall Is It?

antenna
The tip is 1,454 feet (443 meters) above street level. That is as tall as 15 blue whales lined up end to end.

102nd floor observatory
This observatory is 1,250 feet (381 meters) high. That is about as tall as 75 giraffes standing on top of each other.

86th floor observatory
This observatory is 1,050 feet (320 meters) high. That is the height of 105 elephants standing on top of each other.

main entrance
The main entrance of the Empire State Building is at street level.

Picture Glossary

antenna
A wire rod used for sending and receiving radio and television signals.

New York City
The largest city in New York state.

binoculars
An instrument used to make faraway things look closer.

signals
Information carried by radio waves.

elevator
A machine that takes people from one level to another in a building.

symbol
A design, figure, or object that represents something else.

Index

To Learn More

Learning more is as easy as 1, 2, 3.

1) Go to www.factsurfer.com

2) Enter "EmpireStateBuilding" into the search box.

3) Click the "Surf" button to see a list of websites.

With factsurfer.com, finding more information is just a click away.